DOPAMINE DETOX

**7 DAYS PRACTICAL GUIDE TO FREEDOM FROM ALCOHOL
AND PORNOGRAPHY ADDICTION**

By

Rose F. Ryals

- **CULTIVATING A FULFILLING AND BALANCED LIFE BEYOND ADDICTION**

INTRODUCTION

"Dopamine Detox : 7 Days Practical Guide to Freedom from Alcohol and Pornography Addiction" invites you to embark on a transformative journey. Throughout the next week, we'll explore strategies and exercises aimed at breaking free from the powerful hold of alcohol and pornography addiction. This guide is your roadmap to regaining control and rediscovering the joy of authentic, fulfilling experiences. Let's step into a life unburdened by these challenges and work towards a healthier, more balanced existence.

Over the next seven days, you'll delve into actionable steps designed to reset your relationship with dopamine, the neurotransmitter at the heart of these addictions. Through targeted activities, mindful practices, and insightful reflections, you'll gradually shift towards a lifestyle that fosters genuine satisfaction and fulfillment.

Each day of this guide is crafted to empower you, providing a structured approach to tackle the challenges associated with alcohol and pornography. As we navigate this journey together, remember that this is not just about abstaining; it's about cultivating a mindset that appreciates the richness of life beyond these addictive patterns.

Embark on a journey towards a liberated and empowered version of yourself with the Dopamine Detox Guide. Each day is crafted to empower you, providing a structured approach to tackle the challenges associated with alcohol and pornography. This is more than abstaining—it's about cultivating a mindset that appreciates the richness of life beyond these addictive patterns. Let the Dopamine Detox Guide be your companion on this transformative expedition.

CHAPTER 1

UNDERSTANDING THE DOPAMINE CONNECTION

INTRODUCTION TO DOPAMINE: EXPLORING ITS ROLE IN ADDICTION

Dopamine, often referred to as the "feel-good" neurotransmitter, plays a central role in shaping our behaviors, motivations, and the way we experience pleasure. In this chapter, we embark on an enlightening journey into the intricate world of dopamine and its profound connection to addiction.

As we unravel the scientific complexities, we'll delve into how dopamine influences the brain's reward system and contributes to the development and perpetuation of addictive behaviors. Understanding this neurochemical interplay is crucial for anyone seeking freedom from the clutches of alcohol and pornography addiction.

Through this exploration, you'll gain insights into the mechanisms that make these habits so compelling and challenging to overcome. By comprehending the role of dopamine, we lay the foundation for a holistic approach to detoxification, paving the way for a more informed and empowered journey ahead. Let's navigate the fascinating terrain of neurotransmitters and addiction, setting the stage for transformative change.

Moving beyond the biological aspects, we'll also explore the psychological dimensions of addiction tied to dopamine. This includes the ways in which environmental factors, stressors, and emotional triggers intertwine with dopamine release, contributing to the reinforcement of addictive cycles.

Throughout this exploration, keep in mind that knowledge is a powerful tool on the path to recovery. Armed with a deeper understanding of dopamine's intricate dance within our neural pathways, you'll be better equipped to navigate the challenges that lie ahead. The insights gained here will serve as a compass, guiding you towards a more conscious and intentional approach to breaking free from the grip of addiction

As we unravel the mysteries of dopamine's role in addiction, remember that this journey is not just about overcoming challenges but also about discovering the strength within yourself to reclaim control and cultivate a life filled with purpose and genuine satisfaction. Let's delve into the heart of addiction's chemistry, armed with the knowledge needed to embark on a transformative and empowering detoxification process.

THE SCIENCE BEHIND ALCOHOL AND PORNOGRAPHY ADDICTION

In this section, we delve into the intricate scientific underpinnings of alcohol and pornography addiction, understanding how these behaviors become deeply rooted in the neural circuitry of the brain.

It is divided into the following parts:

Neuroplasticity and Addiction

Neuroplasticity, the brain's remarkable ability to adapt and reorganize itself, is a key player in the complex dynamics of addiction. In the context of addictive behaviors associated with alcohol and pornography, understanding neuroplasticity unveils the transformative processes occurring within the brain.

1. Adaptation to Repetitive Behaviors:

Neuroplasticity allows the brain to adapt to repetitive behaviors.Structural and functional changes occur in neural pathways over time.Habits related to addiction become deeply ingrained through this adaptive process.

2. Shaping Habit Formation:

Neuroplasticity plays a crucial role in forming and perpetuating habits.The brain's plastic nature influences the development and persistence of addictive behaviors.Understanding these neural mechanisms is key to addressing addictive habits.

3. Impact on Susceptibility and Recovery:

Individual differences in neuroplasticity contribute to varying susceptibilities to addiction.Recognizing the role of neuroplasticity offers insights into personalized approaches to recovery.Positive harnessing of neuroplasticity becomes a hopeful avenue for breaking the cycle of addiction and fostering recovery.

In essence, neuroplasticity serves as the backdrop for the ongoing dialogue between the brain and addictive behaviors. By unraveling the intricacies of this phenomenon, we gain valuable insights into the malleability of the brain and its potential for change. This understanding becomes a cornerstone in crafting effective strategies for addiction recovery, acknowledging the dynamic nature of the neural landscape on the path to healing.

Dopaminergic Pathways

Dopaminergic pathways are intricate neural circuits crucial in understanding addiction, particularly in the realms of alcohol and pornography. These pathways involve the release and reception of dopamine, a neurotransmitter that plays a central role in the brain's reward system.

1. Specific Pathways:

Dopaminergic pathways, notably the mesolimbic and mesocortical systems, form specific neural circuits implicated in addiction.These pathways play a pivotal role in reinforcing addictive behaviors, contributing to the intricate neural processes associated with substance and behavioral dependencies.

2. Reward Pathways:

Within the dopaminergic pathways, exploration focuses on the intricate reward pathways where dopamine release occurs.Dopamine, acting as the brain's "feel-good" neurotransmitter, shapes the perception of pleasure, creating a reinforcement loop that fuels the desire for rewarding stimuli.

3. Role in Compulsive Behavior:

Delving into the critical role of dopamine in driving compulsive tendencies linked to addiction.Dopamine's influence extends to motivation and decision-making processes, contributing to the challenge individuals face when trying to resist or overcome addictive substances or behaviors.

Understanding these dopaminergic pathways provides a foundational grasp of the physiological mechanisms driving addiction, offering insights into the complexity of the brain's reward system and its role in compulsive behaviors.

EFFECTS ON THE BRAIN AND BEHAVIOR

The interplay between addiction, particularly in the context of alcohol and pornography, manifests profound effects on both the brain and behavior, shaping the intricate relationship between neural processes and actions.

1. Structural Changes in the Brain:

Addiction induces structural alterations in the brain, impacting regions associated with decision-making, impulse control, and reward processing.Long-term exposure to addictive substances or behaviors can lead to changes in neuronal connections and synaptic plasticity.

2. Neurotransmitter Imbalance:

Addiction disrupts the delicate balance of neurotransmitters, including dopamine, serotonin, and GABA.Imbalances contribute to heightened cravings, altered mood states, and challenges in regulating emotional responses.

3. Behavioral Manifestations:

Addiction influences behavior by creating compulsive tendencies, diminishing impulse control, and altering priorities.Individuals may exhibit a heightened drive to seek the addictive substance or behavior, often at the expense of other essential aspects of life.

4. Impaired Decision-Making:

Addiction can impair cognitive functions related to decision-making, leading to choices that prioritize immediate rewards over long-term well-being.Individuals may struggle to weigh the consequences of their actions, perpetuating the cycle of addictive behaviors.

5. Altered Reward Sensitivity:

The brain's reward system undergoes adaptations, resulting in altered sensitivity to natural rewards.This can lead to a decreased ability to experience pleasure from everyday activities, further reinforcing the reliance on the addictive substance or behavior for reward.

6. Emotional Dysregulation:

Addiction contributes to emotional dysregulation, characterized by mood swings, increased stress, and difficulty managing emotions.The altered neurotransmitter balance plays a role in emotional disturbances, creating a challenging environment for maintaining mental well-being.

Understanding these effects on both the brain and behavior underscores the multi-faceted nature of addiction. It emphasizes the importance of holistic interventions that address not only the physiological consequences on the brain but also the behavioral patterns that sustain addictive cycles. Recovery involves navigating this intricate interplay, promoting healing on both neurological and psychological fronts for a comprehensive and sustainable path to well-being.

CHAPTER 2: 7 DAYS DETOX PLAN

DAY 1-2: UNVEILING HABITS AND TRIGGERS

IDENTIFYING PATTERNS AND TRIGGERS ASSOCIATED WITH ADDICTION

Embarking on the first steps of the detox journey involves a focused exploration of existing habits and the triggers that perpetuate addictive behaviors. This phase is crucial in gaining self-awareness and laying the groundwork for targeted intervention.

The initial step in the detoxification process involves a focused effort on identifying patterns associated with addictive behaviors. This self-reflective exploration is crucial for gaining insight into the habits that have become ingrained and understanding the factors that contribute to their persistence.

1. Self-Reflective Exploration:

Engage in introspection to recognize and acknowledge recurring patterns in your behavior.Examine the circumstances, emotions, or thoughts that consistently precede engaging in addictive habits.

2. Behavioral Documentation:

Document instances of addictive behavior to create a tangible record of patterns.Note the frequency, triggers, and contextual factors surrounding these behaviors to discern underlying trends.

3. Recognizing Triggers:

Identify specific triggers that prompt the initiation of addictive actions.Look for commonalities in situations, stressors, or emotional states that consistently precede engagement in alcohol or pornography use.

By meticulously identifying patterns, you pave the way for a deeper understanding of the mechanisms driving addictive behaviors. This awareness becomes a powerful tool for crafting targeted strategies to disrupt established patterns and initiate meaningful change on your journey towards recovery.

Triggers and Associations

Understanding the specific triggers and associations that precede addictive behaviors is a pivotal aspect of the detoxification process. By unraveling the intricacies of these triggers, individuals can gain valuable insights into the emotional, environmental, or situational cues that prompt engagement in alcohol or pornography use.

1. Emotional Triggers:

Identify emotions such as stress, anxiety, or boredom that serve as catalysts for addictive behaviors.Explore the connection between emotional states and the impulse to seek solace or escape through alcohol or pornography.

2. Environmental Cues:

Recognize specific environments or settings that act as triggers for addictive actions.Explore how the presence of certain cues or surroundings may elicit the desire to engage in the familiar patterns of alcohol or pornography use.

3. Situational Prompts:

Uncover situational prompts that consistently lead to the initiation of addictive behaviors.Consider how routine activities or particular circumstances become linked to the inclination to turn to substances or activities for gratification.

4. Cognitive Triggers:

Explore thought patterns or cognitive processes that trigger the desire for addictive behaviors.Identify automatic thoughts or distorted beliefs that contribute to the impulse to engage in alcohol or pornography use.

5. Social Influences:

Examine social contexts and interpersonal dynamics that act as triggers for addictive actions.Recognize the impact of social pressures, peer influence, or specific relationships on the tendency to resort to addictive habits.

6. Temporal Patterns:

Consider temporal patterns, such as specific times of day or recurring situations, that trigger the inclination towards addictive behaviors.Recognize how daily routines or certain time-related cues contribute to the habitual nature of alcohol or pornography consumption.

As you delve into these triggers and associations, you equip yourself with a comprehensive understanding of the diverse factors that contribute to the initiation of addictive behaviors. This knowledge becomes a foundation for developing personalized strategies to mitigate the influence of triggers, fostering resilience and empowerment on your journey towards freedom from addiction.

Mapping Behavioral Chains

Mapping behavioral chains is a crucial step in the detoxification process, offering a detailed exploration of the sequence of actions, thoughts, and emotions that unfold before, during, and after engaging in addictive behaviors. This process helps individuals gain a comprehensive understanding of the interconnected elements that sustain the addictive cycle.

1. Sequence of Actions:

Document the step-by-step sequence of actions leading to the engagement in addictive behaviors.Identify the behaviors that precede, accompany, and follow the use of alcohol or involvement in pornography.

2. Emotional States and Thoughts:

Explore the emotional states experienced throughout the behavioral chain.Document accompanying thoughts, beliefs, or cognitive processes that influence decision-making during each phase.

3. Triggers and Reinforcements:

Highlight the triggers identified in previous reflections and note their role at different points in the chain.Identify reinforcing factors that contribute to the continuation of the behavioral sequence.

4. Environmental Context:

Consider the environmental context in which each phase of the behavioral chain occurs.Note the physical surroundings, social settings, or other contextual elements that play a role in the unfolding of addictive behaviors.

5. Consequences and Aftermath:

Explore the immediate and long-term consequences of engaging in addictive behaviors.Document the emotional, physical, and social outcomes, providing a holistic view of the impact of the behavioral chain.

6. Patterns of Escalation:

Identify any patterns of escalation within the behavioral chain.Examine whether the intensity or frequency of actions increases over time, contributing to a reinforcing cycle.

7. Alternative Responses:

Introduce alternative responses or behaviors that could disrupt the established chain.Consider healthier coping mechanisms or strategies that can be integrated at different points to redirect the course of the behavioral sequence.

8. Reflective Analysis:

Engage in reflective analysis of the mapped behavioral chain.Identify moments of vulnerability, decision points, and opportunities for intervention, fostering a deeper understanding of one's triggers and reactions.

Mapping behavioral chains provides a comprehensive overview of the complexities involved in addictive behaviors. This visual representation becomes a dynamic tool for intervention, allowing individuals to strategically disrupt the sequence, implement positive changes, and cultivate a more intentional and empowered approach to navigating challenges on the path to recovery.

SELF-REFLECTION EXERCISES

Engaging in thoughtful self-reflection is a pivotal aspect of the detoxification journey, fostering awareness and insight into one's thoughts, emotions, and behaviors. These exercises are designed to guide individuals through a process of introspection, aiding in the identification of patterns, triggers, and the motivations behind addictive behaviors.

1. Journaling Prompts:

Encourage regular journaling to explore thoughts, emotions, and daily experiences.Use prompts such as "What emotions am I experiencing right now?" or "Identify situations triggering cravings" to guide the reflective process.

2. Timeline of Cravings:

Create a timeline documenting specific moments of cravings throughout the day.Note accompanying emotions, activities, or environmental factors to discern patterns in the timing and intensity of cravings.

3. Values Clarification:

Reflect on personal values and aspirations.Consider how addictive behaviors align or conflict with these values, prompting contemplation on the significance of aligning actions with core beliefs.

4. Triggers Identification Worksheet:

Utilize a structured worksheet to systematically identify triggers.

Categorize triggers into emotional, environmental, cognitive, and social factors to gain a comprehensive understanding of influential elements.

5. Mindfulness Meditation:

Practice mindfulness meditation to cultivate present-moment awareness.Observe thoughts and sensations without judgment, allowing a deeper understanding of the internal landscape.

6. Goal Setting and Prioritization:

Set short-term and long-term goals related to detoxification.Prioritize these goals to create a roadmap for progress, integrating them into daily reflections to track achievements.

7. Positive Affirmations:

Develop positive affirmations to counter negative thought patterns.Repeat affirmations that reinforce resilience, self-worth, and the capacity for positive change.

Engaging in these self-reflection exercises provides individuals with the tools to navigate the complexities of addiction, promoting self-awareness and empowering them to make intentional choices aligned with their recovery goals.

DAY 3-4: INTRODUCING MINDFUL PRACTICES

INCORPORATING MINDFULNESS INTO DAILY ROUTINE

Integrating mindfulness practices into daily life is a powerful strategy for individuals on the path to recovery. Mindfulness cultivates present-moment awareness, helping to manage stress, regulate emotions, and disrupt automatic responses associated with addictive behaviors. Here's a guide on how to infuse mindfulness into your daily routine:

1. **Morning Mindfulness Ritual:**

Begin the day with a mindful activity, such as mindful breathing or a short meditation.Set positive intentions for the day, fostering a grounded and focused mindset.

2. **Mindful Meals:**

Turn eating into a mindful practice by savoring each bite.Pay attention to the taste, texture, and sensations, fostering a deeper connection with the experience of nourishing your body.

3. **Mindful Movement:**

Incorporate mindful movement, such as yoga or tai chi, into your routine.Focus on the sensations of movement and breath, promoting physical well-being and mental clarity.

4. **Breath Awareness Breaks:**

Take short breaks throughout the day for focused breath awareness.Center yourself by taking a few minutes to observe your breath, promoting relaxation and breaking the cycle of stress.

5. **Mindful Work Practices:**

Infuse mindfulness into work tasks by practicing full attention.Engage fully in each task, appreciating the process rather than being solely outcome-oriented.

6. **Mindful Evening Wind-Down:**

Dedicate time in the evening for a mindful wind-down routine.Reflect on the day with gratitude, and engage in calming activities such as reading or gentle stretching.

7. Mindfulness Before Sleep:

Practice a mindfulness exercise before sleep to ease into restfulness.Guided body scans or progressive relaxation techniques can promote a tranquil state of mind.

8. Mindful Breathing During Challenges:

When faced with challenges or cravings, turn to mindful breathing.Take a few deep, intentional breaths to ground yourself in the present moment, allowing space for thoughtful responses rather than impulsive reactions.

9. Mindful Technology Use:

Be mindful of your technology use, especially with potentially triggering content.Set intentional limits, practice digital detoxes, and use technology mindfully to reduce stress and enhance overall well-being.

10. Mindful Gratitude Practice:

Incorporate a gratitude practice into your routine.Reflect on three things you are grateful for each day, fostering a positive mindset and reinforcing the appreciation for the present moment.

11. Mindful Social Interactions:

Approach social interactions with mindfulness.Listen attentively, be fully present in conversations, and notice the emotions and sensations arising during social engagements.

12. Mindful Nature Connection:

Spend time in nature mindfully.Engage your senses by observing the sights, sounds, and textures around you, fostering a sense of connection and grounding.

13. Mindful Reflection Journal:

Maintain a mindful reflection journal.Regularly jot down moments of mindfulness, insights, and progress in your journey, creating a tangible record of your evolving awareness.

Incorporating mindfulness into various aspects of your daily routine serves as a transformative practice. It not only enhances your ability to navigate challenges associated with addiction but also contributes to an overall sense of wellwell-being, resilience, and purpose in your recovery journey.

TECHNIQUES FOR MANAGING CRAVINGS

Effectively managing cravings is an essential skill on the path to recovery. Employing various techniques can help individuals navigate and overcome the intense urges associated with addiction. Here are strategies to manage cravings:

1. Mindful Awareness:

Cultivate awareness of cravings without judgment.Acknowledge the sensations, thoughts, and emotions without acting on them, creating a space for conscious choice.

2. Deep Breathing:

Practice deep and intentional breathing.Inhale slowly, hold the breath briefly, and exhale fully. This simple technique promotes relaxation and helps to redirect focus away from cravings.

3. Positive Visualization:

Visualize positive outcomes of resisting cravings.Imagine the sense of accomplishment, improved well-being, and progress in your recovery journey, reinforcing motivation to overcome cravings.

4. Behavioral Distraction:

Engage in activities that distract from cravings.Physical exercises, hobbies, or tasks that require concentration can redirect attention away from the urge to engage in addictive behaviors.

5. Mindful Eating:

If the craving is related to substances like alcohol, practice mindful eating.Savor each bite, paying attention to taste, texture, and satisfaction, fostering a mindful relationship with food.

6. Self-Talk and Affirmations:

Use positive self-talk and affirmations.Remind yourself of your commitment to recovery, inner strength, and the ability to withstand cravings without giving in.

7. Grounding Techniques:

Employ grounding techniques to anchor yourself in the present moment.Focus on the sensations of touch, sight, sound, taste, or smell to bring attention away from cravings and into the current reality.

8. Connect with Support:

Reach out to your support network.Talk to a friend, family member, or support group to share your experience and gain encouragement during challenging moments.

9. Mindfulness Meditation:

Practice mindfulness meditation during moments of cravings.Observe the sensations without attachment, allowing the cravings to arise and pass without acting on them.

10. Create a Craving Plan:

Develop a personalized plan for managing cravings.Outline specific strategies, contacts, and activities to turn to when cravings intensify.

11. Progress Reflection:

Reflect on your progress in recovery.Remind yourself of the positive changes, achievements, and reasons why overcoming cravings aligns with your broader goals.

By incorporating these techniques into your repertoire, you equip yourself with a diverse set of tools for managing cravings. These strategies not only help you navigate challenging moments but also contribute to the cultivation of resilience and a sense of control on your journey towards recovery.

DAY 5-6: BUILDING HEALTHY ALTERNATIVES

ESTABLISHING POSITIVE HABITS TO REPLACE ADDICTIVE BEHAVIORS

Replacing addictive behaviors with positive habits is a transformative step in the recovery process. By intentionally fostering constructive routines, individuals can create a foundation for lasting change. Here are strategies for establishing positive habits:

1. Identify Trigger-Free Activities:

Identify activities that are free from triggers associated with addictive behaviors.Choose hobbies or pursuits that align with your interests and promote a sense of fulfillment without the risk of triggering cravings.

2. Set Realistic Goals:

Establish realistic and achievable goals for habit formation.Break down larger goals into smaller, manageable steps to build a sense of accomplishment and maintain motivation.

3. Morning Routine Reinforcement:

Incorporate positive habits into your morning routine.Engage in activities such as exercise, meditation, or gratitude practices to set a positive tone for the day.

4. Mindful Exercise:

Integrate regular exercise into your routine.Choose activities that you enjoy and that contribute to physical well-being, promoting a natural release of endorphins.

5. Healthy Nutrition Practices:

Focus on cultivating healthy nutrition habits.Prioritize balanced meals and snacks to support overall well-being and provide stable energy levels throughout the day.

6. Mindful Relaxation Techniques:

Incorporate mindful relaxation techniques into your daily schedule.Practices such as deep breathing, progressive muscle relaxation, or guided imagery can help manage stress and prevent triggers.

7. Learn a New Skill:

Engage in activities that involve learning a new skill.This not only provides a sense of accomplishment but also occupies your mind with positive challenges.

8. Cultivate Social Connections:

Foster positive social connections.Spend time with supportive friends and family, or consider joining social groups aligned with your interests to build a healthy support network.

9. Regular Sleep Patterns:

Prioritize regular and sufficient sleep.Establish a consistent sleep routine to enhance overall well-being and support emotional regulation.

10. Mindful Media Consumption:

Be mindful of your media consumption.Choose content that aligns with positive values and contributes to your well-being, avoiding material that may trigger cravings.

11. Practice Gratitude:

Incorporate a gratitude practice into your daily routine.Reflect on things you are thankful for, fostering a positive mindset and reinforcing the importance of positive habits.

12. Journaling for Reflection:

Maintain a journal for reflection.Document your progress, insights, and positive experiences as you establish and reinforce new, healthy habits.

By intentionally integrating these positive habits into your daily life, you not only create a supportive environment for recovery but also contribute to the overall enhancement of your well-being. These habits serve as constructive alternatives, fostering resilience and reinforcing the positive changes you are making on your journey.

FINDING JOY IN NEW ACTIVITIES

Discovering joy in new activities is a pivotal aspect of the recovery journey, providing positive experiences that can replace and outweigh the allure of addictive behaviors. Here are strategies for finding joy in new activities:

1. Explore Diverse Hobbies:

Try out a variety of hobbies and activities to discover what resonates with you.From art and music to sports and outdoor adventures, exploring diverse interests can unveil unexpected sources of joy.

2. Mindful Engagement:

Engage in activities mindfully, focusing on the present moment.Whether it's taking a nature walk, cooking a new recipe, or practicing a creative outlet, immerse yourself fully in the experience to enhance the sense of joy.

3. Set Achievable Goals:

Set achievable goals related to new activities.Breaking down larger goals into smaller, attainable steps can foster a sense of accomplishment and boost motivation.

4. Join Social Groups:

Participate in social groups or clubs that align with your interests.Connecting with like-minded individuals not only enhances the joy of the activity but also builds a supportive community.

5. Celebrate Small Wins:

Celebrate small wins and milestones in your exploration of new activities.Acknowledging your progress reinforces the positive impact of engaging in joyful pursuits.

6. Embrace Creativity:

Embrace your creative side.Activities such as writing, drawing, or crafting can be both expressive outlets and sources of joy, allowing you to tap into your imagination.

7. Attend Events and Workshops:

Attend events or workshops related to your interests.Immersing yourself in the community and learning from others can enhance the joy derived from the activity.

8. Mindful Presence in Nature:

Spend time in nature with mindful presence.Whether it's hiking, gardening, or simply enjoying a park, connecting with nature can bring a profound sense of joy and tranquility.

9. Mix Solo and Social Activities:

Balance solo activities with social engagements.Finding joy in both solitary pursuits and shared experiences allows for a diverse and fulfilling range of activities.

10. Learn Something New:

Challenge yourself to learn something new regularly.The process of acquiring new skills or knowledge not only stimulates joy but also fosters a sense of personal growth.

11. Express Yourself Through Movement:

Incorporate movement into your activities.Dance, yoga, or other forms of physical expression can be joyful outlets for self-expression and well-being.

12. Practice Gratitude:

Cultivate gratitude for the joy found in new activities.Regularly reflect on the positive impact these pursuits have on your overall mood and outlook.

By actively seeking and embracing joy in new activities, you not only create positive alternatives to addictive behaviors but also enhance your overall quality of life. These joyful experiences contribute to a sense of fulfillment, reinforcing the positive changes you are making on your journey to recovery.

DAY 7: REFLECTION AND FUTURE PLANNING

ASSESSING PROGRESS AND ACHIEVEMENTS

Regularly assessing your progress and acknowledging achievements is a crucial part of the recovery journey. This reflection not only provides a sense of accomplishment but also helps guide future efforts. Here are steps for effectively assessing progress and celebrating achievements:

1. Establish Clear Goals:

Define clear and measurable goals for your recovery journey.Having specific objectives provides a foundation for assessing progress and identifying achievements.

2. Regular Self-Reflection:

Engage in regular self-reflection.Set aside dedicated time to reflect on your journey, examining both challenges and successes.

3. Celebrate Small Wins:

Acknowledge and celebrate small victories along the way.Recognizing even the smallest positive steps reinforces motivation and resilience.

4. Tracking Milestones:

Create a system for tracking milestones.Whether through a journal, calendar, or digital tool, document significant moments and achievements to visually observe your progress.

5. Evaluate Challenges:

Assess challenges objectively.Understand the obstacles you've encountered and consider the lessons learned, emphasizing growth and resilience.

6. Seek Feedback:

Seek feedback from your support network.Valuable insights from friends, family, or professionals can provide an external perspective on your progress.

7. Adjust Goals as Needed:

Be flexible in adjusting goals as needed.If circumstances change or new insights emerge, adapt your goals to remain realistic and relevant.

8. Mindful Gratitude Practice:

Incorporate a gratitude practice into your assessment routine.Express gratitude for the positive changes and progress you've experienced, fostering a positive mindset.

9. Review Coping Strategies:

Evaluate the effectiveness of coping strategies.Identify which strategies have been most helpful in managing cravings and challenges, refining your toolkit for future use.

10. Document Emotional Well-Being:

Document changes in emotional well-being.Pay attention to shifts in mood, stress levels, and overall mental health as indicators of progress.

11. Set New Challenges:

Consider setting new challenges.As you achieve goals, introducing new challenges ensures continued growth and engagement in the recovery process.

12. Celebrate Milestones:

Celebrate significant milestones.Whether it's a month, six months, or a year of progress, commemorate these milestones as markers of achievement.

Regularly assessing progress and celebrating achievements serves as a motivational tool, reinforcing the positive impact of your efforts. This reflective process not only highlights the strides made in your recovery journey but also provides valuable insights for continued growth and success.

DEVELOPING A SUSTAINABLE PLAN FOR THE FUTURE

Creating a sustainable plan for the future is essential in maintaining the progress achieved in your recovery journey. Here are steps to guide the development of a plan that ensures long-term well-being:

1. Reflect on Values and Priorities:

Begin by reflecting on your core values and priorities.Identify aspects of life that align with your values and contribute to overall well-being.

2. Define Long-Term Goals:

Define clear and achievable long-term goals.These goals should encompass various aspects of your life, including health, relationships, personal development, and career aspirations.

3. Break Goals into Actionable Steps:

Break down long-term goals into smaller, actionable steps.This approach makes the journey more manageable and allows for a sense of progress along the way.

4. Incorporate Healthy Habits:

Embed healthy habits into your routine.Ensure that positive practices related to nutrition, exercise, sleep, and mindfulness become integral parts of your daily life.

5. Maintain Support Systems:

Nurture and maintain your support systems.Continue to engage with friends, family, or support groups that have been instrumental in your recovery, fostering a sense of community.

6. Adopt Lifelong Learning:

Embrace a mindset of lifelong learning.Continue to explore new interests, acquire knowledge, and challenge yourself intellectually for ongoing personal development.

7. Stress Management Strategies:

Develop and implement effective stress management strategies.Identify techniques that work for you, whether it's mindfulness, relaxation exercises, or other stress-reducing activities.

8. Regular Self-Assessment:

Incorporate regular self-assessment into your routine.Periodically review your progress, reassess goals, and make adjustments based on evolving priorities and circumstances.

9. Financial Planning:

Include financial planning in your sustainable future plan.Establish financial goals, budgeting practices, and savings plans to ensure stability and reduce stress.

10. Career Development:

Consider your career path and professional development. – Identify opportunities for growth, skill enhancement, or even potential career changes that align with your long-term objectives.

11. Cultivate Healthy Relationships:

Cultivate and maintain healthy relationships. – Foster connections that contribute positively to your well-being, emphasizing open communication and mutual support.

12. Regular Health Checkups:

Prioritize regular health checkups. – Consistent monitoring of physical and mental health is vital for early detection and intervention.

13. Embrace Flexibility: -

Embrace flexibility in your plan. – Recognize that life is dynamic, and your plan should adapt to changing circumstances while remaining aligned with your overarching values and goals.

Developing a sustainable plan for the future involves a holistic approach that integrates various aspects of well-being. This comprehensive strategy ensures that your recovery journey not only continues but thrives, fostering a fulfilling and purposeful life.

CHAPTER 3: SUSTAINING A DOPAMINE-HEALTHY LIFESTYLE

POST-DETOX STRATEGIES: MAINTAINING PROGRESS

Transitioning from detox to maintaining progress is a critical phase in the recovery journey. These strategies focus on sustaining the positive changes made during detoxification and fortifying your commitment to long-term well-being:

1. Establish a Support Network:

Cultivate a robust support network that understands your journey.Surround yourself with individuals who offer encouragement, understanding, and positivity.

2. Engage in Ongoing Therapy:

Continue therapy or counseling as needed.Regular sessions provide a structured space for addressing challenges, exploring personal growth, and maintaining emotional well-being.

3. Develop Healthy Routines:

Solidify healthy daily routines.Consistency in activities such as sleep, exercise, and meals contributes to stability and reinforces positive habits.

4. Mindfulness Practices:

Integrate mindfulness practices into daily life.Mindful awareness helps manage stress, enhances resilience, and fosters a deeper connection with the present moment.

5. Regular Check-Ins with Professionals:

Schedule regular check-ins with healthcare professionals.Ensure ongoing monitoring of physical and mental health to address any emerging issues promptly.

6. Celebrate Sobriety Milestones:

Celebrate milestones in your sobriety journey.Acknowledge and commemorate achievements, whether it's a week, a month, or a year of sustained progress.

7. Expand Social Connections:

Expand your social connections with others in recovery.Join support groups, participate in sober activities, and build a broader community that shares common goals.

8. Address Co-occurring Issues:

Address any co-occurring mental health issues.If there are underlying mental health concerns, seek appropriate professional help to ensure comprehensive care.

9. Educate Yourself:

Stay informed about addiction, recovery, and mental health.Continuous education empowers you with knowledge and equips you to navigate challenges with a deeper understanding

10. Set New Goals: -

Establish new goals and aspirations. – Setting fresh objectives provides a sense of purpose and direction, promoting ongoing personal development.

11. Embrace a Healthy Lifestyle:

Embrace a holistic and healthy lifestyle. – Prioritize nutritious eating, regular exercise, and self-care practices to support your overall well-being.

12. Recognize Warning Signs: -

Be vigilant for warning signs of relapse. – Develop strategies to recognize and manage triggers, and have a plan in place to seek support if needed.

13. Express Gratitude: -

Cultivate a gratitude practice. – Regularly express gratitude for the positive changes and progress you've experienced, reinforcing a positive mindset.

14. Emphasize Self-Compassion:

Practice self-compassion. – Be kind to yourself during challenging moments, understanding that setbacks are part of the journey, and learning and growth continue.

By implementing these post-detox strategies, you create a resilient framework for maintaining progress. This ongoing commitment to well-being ensures that your recovery journey remains a dynamic and fulfilling process, supporting a life of purpose and sustained positive change.

PREVENTING RELAPSE AND OVERCOMING SETBACKS

Preventing relapse and navigating setbacks is an integral part of the recovery journey. These strategies are designed to empower individuals to proactively manage challenges and maintain their commitment to sobriety:

- Develop a Relapse Prevention Plan:

Create a detailed relapse prevention plan with specific strategies and coping mechanisms.Clearly outline warning signs, triggers, and concrete steps to take in the event of increased vulnerability.

- Identify and Address Triggers:

Identify personal triggers that may lead to cravings or relapse.Once recognized, develop healthy alternatives or coping strategies to address these triggers proactively.

- Stay Connected to Support Systems:

Maintain strong connections with your support network.Regular communication with friends, family, or support groups provides crucial encouragement during challenging times.

- Regular Self-Reflection:

Engage in regular self-reflection.Assess emotional states, stress levels, and potential triggers, allowing for early intervention and adjustment of coping strategies.

- Mindfulness Practices:

Integrate mindfulness practices into daily life.Mindfulness helps cultivate awareness of thoughts and emotions, providing a foundation for making conscious choices in response to challenges.

- Learn from Setbacks:

View setbacks as learning opportunities.Analyze the circumstances surrounding setbacks, identify contributing factors, and use this knowledge to refine your relapse prevention plan.

- Seek Professional Guidance:

Reach out to healthcare professionals or therapists.Seeking guidance during challenging times can provide valuable insights and support tailored to your specific needs.

- **Reassess and Adjust Goals:**

Reassess long-term goals and make necessary adjustments.Flexibility in goal-setting ensures alignment with evolving priorities and reduces potential frustration.

- **Healthy Coping Mechanisms:**

Cultivate a repertoire of healthy coping mechanisms.Identify activities, hobbies, or relaxation techniques that provide alternative outlets for stress and emotional regulation.

- **Regular Check-Ins:**

Schedule regular check-ins with your healthcare team. – Consistent monitoring of physical and mental health ensures a proactive approach to any emerging issues.

- **Engage in Regular Physical Activity:**

Prioritize regular physical activity. – Exercise not only contributes to overall well-being but also serves as a positive outlet for stress and tension.

- **Celebrate Progress:**

Celebrate ongoing progress. – Acknowledge and celebrate the positive changes and achievements, reinforcing the motivation to continue on the path of recovery.

- **Build Resilience: -**

Focus on building resilience. – Cultivate a mindset that views setbacks as temporary obstacles rather than insurmountable challenges, fostering adaptability and perseverance.

- **Emphasize Self-Care:**

Prioritize self-care practices. – Regular self-care contributes to emotional well-being, reducing vulnerability to stressors that may contribute to relapse.

- **Reconnect with Supportive Activities:**

Reconnect with activities that bring joy and fulfillment. – Engaging in positive and enjoyable pursuits reinforces the sense of purpose and provides an antidote to potential setbacks.

By incorporating these strategies, individuals enhance their ability to prevent relapse and effectively overcome setbacks. This proactive and holistic approach supports ongoing recovery and reinforces the commitment to a life of sobriety and well-being.

CULTIVATING A FULFILLING AND BALANCED LIFE BEYOND ADDICTION

Transitioning beyond addiction involves not only maintaining sobriety but also creating a life filled with purpose, joy, and balance. Here are strategies for cultivating a fulfilling and balanced life beyond addiction:

1. Discover Personal Passions:

Explore and discover personal passions and interests.Engaging in activities that bring genuine joy and fulfillment contributes to a sense of purpose beyond addiction.

2. Build Healthy Relationships:

Cultivate healthy and supportive relationships.Prioritize connections that uplift, inspire, and contribute positively to your well-being.

3. Establish Boundaries:

Set and maintain healthy boundaries in all areas of life.Clearly define limits that protect your well-being and foster balanced relationships.

4. Pursue Continuous Learning:

Embrace a mindset of continuous learning.Pursue educational opportunities, whether formal or informal, to stimulate intellectual growth and personal development.

5. Contribute to Community:

Find ways to contribute to your community.Volunteering or participating in community initiatives fosters a sense of purpose and connection.

6. Prioritize Physical Health:

Prioritize physical health through regular exercise and a balanced diet.Physical well-being is integral to overall life satisfaction and resilience.

7. Embrace Mindfulness Practices:

Incorporate mindfulness practices into daily life.Mindfulness promotes present-moment awareness, reducing stress and enhancing overall mental well-being.

8. Establish a Healthy Work-Life Balance:

Strive for a healthy work-life balance.Prioritize time for relaxation, leisure, and personal pursuits alongside professional responsibilities.

9. Set Realistic Goals:

Set realistic and achievable personal and professional goals.Breaking down larger goals into manageable steps ensures a sense of progress and accomplishment.

10. Engage in Creative Outlets:

Express creativity through various outlets. – Whether it's art, writing, music, or other forms of expression, engaging in creative pursuits enriches life beyond addiction.

11. Practice Gratitude:

Cultivate a gratitude practice. – Regularly reflecting on and expressing gratitude for the positive aspects of life enhances overall well-being.

12. Stay Connected with Support: -

Maintain connections with your support network. – Ongoing communication with friends, family, or support groups ensures continued encouragement and shared celebrations.

13. Enjoy Nature: -

Spend time in nature regularly. – Connecting with the outdoors promotes relaxation, reduces stress, and contributes to a sense of balance.

14. Celebrate Milestones:

Celebrate personal milestones and achievements. – Acknowledge and commemorate your progress, reinforcing a positive self-image and motivation for continued growth.

15. Regularly Evaluate and Adjust:

Regularly evaluate your life and make necessary adjustments. – Flexibility in adapting to changing circumstances ensures ongoing alignment with your evolving values and aspirations.

By integrating these strategies into your post-recovery life, you not only maintain sobriety but also build a foundation for a fulfilling and balanced existence. Cultivating a life beyond addiction involves continuous self-discovery, intentional choices, and a commitment to well-being, ultimately leading to a future filled with purpose and satisfaction.

CONCLUSION: EMBRACING A LIFE BEYOND ADDICTION

In concluding this journey of exploration and transformation, remember that recovery is not just about overcoming addiction; it's about rediscovering life's richness and building a future filled with purpose. As you navigate the challenges and triumphs, embrace the profound truth that your journey is uniquely yours, a tapestry woven with resilience, self-discovery, and the unwavering commitment to a brighter tomorrow.

The path to sobriety extends beyond mere abstinence; it extends towards the creation of a life brimming with fulfillment, balance, and

Authentic joy. Each step you take, every choice you make, contributes to the vibrant mosaic of your newfound reality. Cultivate gratitude for the journey, recognizing that setbacks are not defeats but stepping stones towards personal growth.

As you step into the realm beyond addiction, carry with you the invaluable lessons learned, the strength unearthed in moments of vulnerability, and the unwavering belief in your capacity to craft a life of significance. Stay connected with your support network, savor the victories, and face challenges with the resilience you've cultivated.

At the end of this 7-day journey, let it be a celebration of your resilience, a testament to the power of transformation, and a proclamation that a life beyond addiction is not just possible—it's waiting for you to shape it. Your story is one of triumph, an inspiring narrative that extends far beyond these pages. May your journey continue to unfold, and may each chapter be a testament to the boundless possibilities that await when one chooses the path of recovery.

Printed in Great Britain
by Amazon

44544376R00030